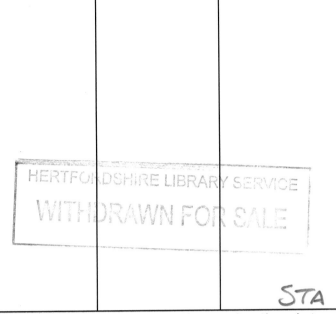
Please renew or return items by the date shown on your receipt

www.hertsdirect.org/libraries

| Renewals and enquiries: | 0300 123 4049 |
| Textphone for hearing or speech impaired | 0300 123 4041 |

D0276120

521 607 14

KEEPING SAFE

ON THE STREET

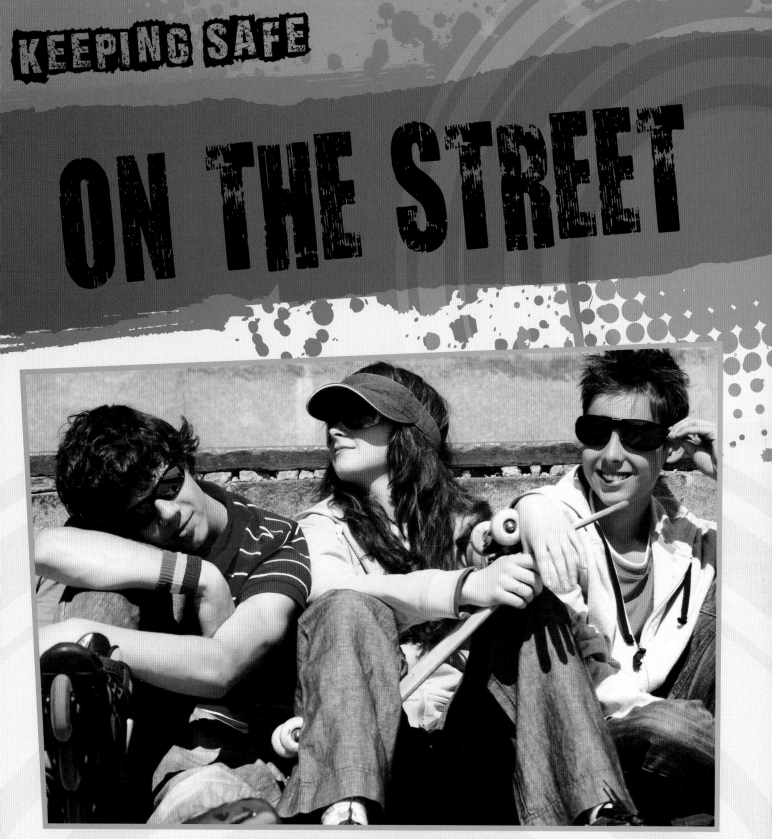

by Honor Head

W
FRANKLIN WATTS
LONDON • SYDNEY

First published in 2014 by Franklin Watts

Copyright © Arcturus Holdings Limited

Franklin Watts
338 Euston Road
London NW1 3BH
Franklin Watts Australia
Level 17/207 Kent Street, Sydney NSW 2000

Produced by Arcturus Publishing Limited,
26/27 Bickels Yard, 151–153 Bermondsey Street, London SE1 3HA

Editors: Penny Worms and Joe Harris
Designer: Emma Randall
Cover designer: Emma Randall
Original design concept: Elaine Wilkinson

Picture credits: All images courtesy of Shutterstock except main image page 26:
Ron Nickel/Design Pics/Corbis.

A CIP catalogue record for this book is available from the British Library.

Dewey Decimal Classification Number 613.6

ISBN 978 1 4451 3248 8

Printed in China

Franklin Watts is a division of Hachette Children's Books,
an Hachette UK company.

www.hachette.co.uk

SL004066UK
Supplier 03 Date 0614, Print Run 3439

CONTENTS

BE STREET SMART

Whether you live in a large city or town, or a quiet country village, you need to be street smart during the day and at night. Being street smart is being aware of what is going on around you and keeping yourself and your belongings safe.

When you're out with friends, stay together. If you want to go somewhere by yourself, tell one of your friends and ask them to wait for you.

Staying safe on the street is not just about being aware of strangers or **muggers**, it's about spotting unexpected dangers before they happen. This includes being aware of what's happening on the road, avoiding dangerous places and using general common sense at **level crossings** or when riding a bike. It also involves being careful around dogs and using your **instincts** about other people.

SAFETY TIP

Even without credit on your phone, you can call the emergency services. Dial 999 in the event of a fire, crime, or if someone is seriously hurt. Only dial 999 in an emergency.

It's great to be out with friends and have the freedom to decide where you go and what you do. But always let an adult at home know where you are and when to expect you back. If you have a mobile, keep some safety numbers on speed dial. As well as your home number, have the phone number of a trusted family member or friend who lives close by.

It's not smart to keep where you are going from your parents. They need to know that you're safe.

KNOW YOUR JOURNEY

When going somewhere new, make sure you know exactly how to get there. Write down instructions before you start your journey. If you are prepared, you will feel and look more confident. And if you take a wrong turning, you should be able to get back on the right track again. Never go with anyone who says they will show you the way.

It helps to plan your journey before you set out. Check out the train and bus times. When walking, avoid shortcuts you don't know and never take a badly lit alleyway or **subway**. Take the phone number of the place where you're going, so you can call if you get lost. And if you need directions, ask a traffic warden or police officer, or go into a shop, bank or library for help.

It is easy to have an accident walking along using your mobile. Stop somewhere safe if you need to look up anything.

SAFETY TIP

When you are on holiday, keep the name and address of where you're staying on you in case you need it.

Leave enough time for your journey. When rushing, you're more likely to take risks crossing the road. Cross somewhere safe, at traffic lights or a zebra crossing if there is one. Never cross between parked cars because they block your view of the road. Don't forget to keep a lookout for bikes.

Don't wear earphones or chat on your mobile when you're crossing the road. You need your eyes and your ears to cross safely.

STAY AWARE

Don't make yourself an easy target for thieves. Walking along with your head down, paying no attention to your surroundings, makes you an ideal victim. Beat any trouble before it starts by looking confident and staying aware. Keep your head up and use your eyes and ears to stay alert to what is happening around you.

Pickpockets and bag snatchers love busy places, so avoid walking along holding your mobile or iPod. Keep your bag closed and make sure nothing valuable is poking out of the top. Keeping your bag close to your body will put off anyone from even trying to steal from you.

When you get something from your bag, zip it up straight away.

SAFETY TIP

If you're lucky enough to get a great new gadget, don't show it off to anyone you don't know well. If you do, you might not have it for long! Always keep **valuables** safe and keep yourself protected from anyone who might want to steal them from you.

If someone does grab your stuff, don't get into a fight because you could get hurt. Let them take it and immediately go to a **safe place** or tell a responsible adult so they can report the crime for you. The non-emergency number for the police is 101. You should never call 999 unless a crime is still happening.

If you're out shopping with friends you might not notice someone taking your bag or coat. Always keep your personal belongings where you can see them.

DOG DANGERS

Most dogs on the street are well behaved with responsible owners, but some dogs can be **aggressive** or nervous of people they don't know. Always take care with unknown dogs. If you're taking a dog out, make sure it is well trained and that you know how to handle it.

Do not touch unknown dogs unless you have asked the owner's permission. If the owner says it's okay, always offer the dog your hand to sniff first so it knows you are friendly. If people stop to stroke your pet, make sure you're not being distracted while someone else tries to take your bag or other belongings. Do not allow strangers to feed your dog. Just say no politely – dog lovers will understand.

Always keep your dog on a lead when you are on the pavement or near traffic.

SAFETY TIP

If you see a stray dog or a dog off its lead, don't touch it. If you are concerned about the animal, speak to an adult about contacting the RSPCA.

If you're out and you see a dog in a front garden, do not touch it even if it looks friendly. Dogs are very protective of their **territory**. Some dogs bark, growl or bare their teeth to show they are protecting their homes – but not all do. So, respect their territory and leave them alone.

Remember, even small, cute-looking dogs can snap and bite if they are frightened by a stranger.

11

STRANGER DANGER

Many strangers are nice, helpful people. However, some strangers can be dangerous. Strangers who are a threat can be young or old, male or female. It's often very difficult to judge who are the 'bad' strangers, so act safely with all strangers.

If someone asks you for help, suggest he or she tries a police officer or another adult. Don't get caught up in conversation no matter how friendly they seem. Do not lend strangers your mobile phone or give them money. If someone follows you, cross the road. If they still follow, go to a safe place and call the police.

If you feel threatened on the street, head for a safe place such as a shop, bank, library, supermarket or post office and tell someone who works there.

SAFETY TIP

If a stranger tries to befriend you, tell a parent or an adult who you trust. If a stranger approaches you near your school, tell a teacher or other staff member.

If a stranger tries to grab you, remember to do this – 'Yell, Run, Tell!' Shout out 'No!' or 'Leave me alone.' Make it as loud as you can. If someone you know is nearby, run to them. If not, run to a busy place, or somewhere that you know there will be people, such as a shop. Tell a trusted adult what has happened.

If you need help, ask a **safe** person such as a police officer, traffic warden, shopkeeper or librarian.

TROUBLE ON THE STREETS

When kids hang around street corners, they sometimes like to show off to others. They may shout insults and cause trouble and it's often best just to ignore them. However, it can be very frightening if someone confronts you. Sometimes they might be drunk or they may have a mental illness. Either way, the best people to deal with them are the police, so get away as quickly as you can.

Walk past a gang on the outside edge of the pavement – you don't want to be trapped or surrounded by them.

If an individual in a group is trying to impress the others, he or she will pick on someone who looks like an easy target. Walk tall and look confident and strong, but don't look as if you want a fight. Don't stare at them but don't scurry past either. Look like you're not someone they want to mess with and they probably won't!

SAFETY TIP

Try to learn a few self-defence moves by joining a club at school or look for a class online. As well as good exercise, it will make you feel more confident.

If someone on the street shouts **abuse**, do not respond. If they are being really aggressive, try to keep out of their way. Turn around and walk in the opposite direction. Head to where you know there are people and shops.

If someone from school is bullying you outside of school, report it. Even if you are away from school when it happens, teachers will still do something about it.

SAFE CYCLING

Before you ride your bike on the streets, make sure you understand the rules of the road. Ask at school or look online for a 'Bikeability' training course. Cycling will be easier, safer and a lot more fun if you know what you're doing.

Always wear a well-fitting helmet and tighten the strap so it doesn't wobble about when you are cycling.

Before you leave the house make sure your bike is **roadworthy**. You should have lights, which should be checked each time you go out. Cycle in bike lanes if possible. Try not to cycle on pavements, unless it's really necessary, especially if they are busy. You could injure yourself and others. When it is dark, wear a reflective jacket so other road users can see you.

Wherever you leave your bike, make sure it is locked up properly and keep the key safe! Leave your bike somewhere that is well lit and busy so you feel safe locking and unlocking it.

Most cycle lanes and roads are kept clean, but keep a look out on the ground in front of you as well as on the road ahead. For example, wet leaves, uneven roads and rubbish in the road could cause your bike to swerve or crash. Watch out for dogs and young children running into the road, especially from behind parked cars.

If you are cycling along a road of parked cars, beware of car doors suddenly swinging open.

SAFE SKATEBOARDING

Skateboarding is a fun activity but with speed comes the possibility of injury. Practise in a safe place such as a skatepark if you can. Chat to your local sports shop about the right equipment and clothing, such as a helmet, pads and shoes, or go online and have a look at some specialist sites.

If you're boarding in a park or public place, clear the area of twigs, leaves and rubbish that might get caught in your wheels. Don't skate where there are many people – it's no fun for you and someone could get hurt. And if you're running out of energy, stop. You are more likely to hurt yourself if you're tired.

The best place to board is a skatepark. It will have proper ramps kept in a safe condition.

SAFETY TIP

If you feel you are going to fall, crouch down and roll off the board commando-style onto your side or bottom. Wearing wrist guards reduces the chances of breaking a wrist or arm, should you need to put your hands down.

Watch and learn how others do the awesome jumps and practise till you get it right. Soon, someone will be watching and learning from you.

Don't be persuaded by other boarders to do stuff that doesn't feel safe, such as skating on street railings or walls. And only do jumps when you're ready. Your skateboard time is for you to have fun and do what you feel comfortable with. You don't have to prove yourself to anyone.

KEEP AWAY FROM BUILDING SITES

Building sites are high-risk danger areas. All kinds of accidents can happen, such as being burnt by chemicals, or injured or trapped by falling materials. Most building sites are private property so going on one is **trespassing**, which is against the law.

It's not worth taking a dare from your friends to go onto a building site. It's dangerous and you won't look very daring if you're being rushed to hospital. If your friends decide to go on a site, stay outside. If they start to do anything stupid, such as climbing scaffolding or switching on machinery, leave and tell an adult.

You must tell an adult if your friends start to mess around on a building site. You could be saving them from serious injury or even death.

SAFETY TIP

Never feel that you have to do what your friends tell you to do. If you know something is dangerous, it is braver to say so and walk away than feel you have to prove yourself to your friends.

There are many hazards on a building site – covered holes that you could fall through, chemicals and sharp objects lying round. These can cause all kinds of nasty injuries. If your friends want to meet on a building site, don't be afraid to say no and to suggest somewhere else, such as a park or skatepark or someone's house.

Signs such as this are there to protect you. You could end up in hospital or in court if you ignore them.

⚠️

Construction site
Keep out

KEEP AWAY FROM RAIL TRACKS

Take extra care around trains, railway stations, train crossings and rail tracks. Trains travel very fast and they cannot stop suddenly – it can take the length of 20 football pitches for a train to come to a halt. Modern trains are fast and quiet. You may not hear or see them until it is too late.

Walking along rail tracks is very dangerous, and not just because of trains. In some places, the rail tracks have a powerful electric current running through them.

Never walk along a railway track, take a shortcut across a track or play on railway lines. You may not hear or see a train until it's too late because most modern trains don't make much noise. If you do see a train and start to run, you could trip and the train will not be able to stop in time.

Always cross railway tracks at a proper railway or level crossing, bridge or **underpass**. Never think you have time to cross if the lights are flashing.

Dropping things onto a train from a railway bridge, or putting anything on the track, is a serious offence. It causes delays, damage to trains and tracks, and can kill people. If you see people doing this, tell an adult.

SAFETY TIP

At a level crossing, if a train goes by and the warning sign still says wait, another train may be right behind. Never cross until the warning light stops.

23

STAY SAFE ON PUBLIC TRANSPORT

Public transport is one of the best ways to get around but stay aware and keep safe. Always check the time of your train or bus so you don't have to wait in a public place for a long time. Choose to wait at busy bus stops or train stations if you have a choice. You'll feel safer with people around.

At train stations, never stand too close to the edge of the platform, and always look where you're going. Put your phone away as this could distract you when you are getting on or off. You could miss your footing or bump into others. If you're travelling alone, avoid getting into an empty carriage. Choose one with lots of people, especially families.

Keep your bag on your lap and hold it close to you. Try to stay aware of what's going on even if you have your earphones in.

24

SAFETY TIP

Take care when getting off a bus. Wait until the bus has pulled away and you can see the road clearly before crossing.

Often you'll be taking public transport with friends. You will probably feel safe in their company, but being distracted can make you careless. Don't go too close to the curb at the bus stop or start messing around. It only takes a second off-balance to cause an accident. On a fast-moving train or bus, it's dangerous to throw anything out of the window, or to stick your head or hands out.

Being street smart enables you to be independent and to feel confident when travelling on your own or with friends.

AFTER DARK

When it gets dark early, just follow a few extra rules to stay safe. If you are walking home from school in the dark, always try to walk with friends and choose a well-lit, busy route. If you're going out and about, tell your parents where you are and when to expect you home.

If you have to wait for friends or for public transport, stand somewhere that is busy and well lit. Never, ever accept a lift from someone you don't know well, even if they know your name and say they know your parents. If you are in any doubt, phone home first and check it's okay.

If a car stops and someone asks for directions, don't get close to the car even if they ask you to look at a map.

SAFETY TIP

If you have to travel after dark, take a small torch with a very bright light. Use it to light your way. Discuss carrying a safety alarm with your parents, local police or school.

If you are out after dark, avoid dark alleys and empty subways. Walk in the middle of the pavement where you are safe from the road. If you think a person or car is following you, head straight for a bright busy place or a well-lit house and ask for help.

When out with friends after dark, stick together and look out for one another. Don't go into a dark park or take a shortcut across open spaces.

SUMMARIZER

Here's a reminder of the most important points made in the book. Look back if you want to see more information about anything.

1 Always let someone know where you are going and when you'll be back.

2 Keep any valuables in a bag or pocket and don't flash new gadgets around.

3 Stay alert to dangers when you are crossing the road – you need both eyes and ears to be safe.

4 Only take your dog out alone if it is well trained. Don't touch or feed unknown dogs.

5 If you think someone is following you, or if anyone tries to grab you, yell and run to the nearest safe place.

6 Walk with confidence. If someone is rude or aggressive to you, don't respond. Just walk away.

7 When cycling on the roads, make sure your bike is roadworthy and that you are wearing protective and reflective clothing.

8 If you are a skateboarder, go to a well-kept skatepark, wear protective gear, and learn how to fall to avoid breaking a wrist or arm.

9 Building sites, railway tracks and road works are dangerous places – stay away!

10 On public transport sit with others and wait at well-lit, busy stops or stations.

11 In the dark, walk along well-lit roads and never take short cuts down empty alleys or across open spaces.

12 If a car driver stops to talk to you, even if it's to ask directions, don't go near the car.

GLOSSARY

abuse unfair, cruel or violent treatment of someone

aggressive angry, and behaving in a threatening way

instincts feelings you have about a person, place or situation that you can't explain. Sometimes your instincts may tell you if a person is good or bad.

level crossing a crossing across a railway track for people on foot and in cars, usually with a gate and signal lights

muggers thieves who attack you to steal your things

roadworthy when a vehicle is safe to go on the roads

safe person a person you should tell if you are afraid, upset or lost on the street, such as a police officer, traffic warden or someone working in a shop, bank, doctors' surgery or library

safe place a place to go if you need help while you are out, such as a library, bank, police station, shop or supermarket

subway a tunnel under a road for people on foot

territory an area or place where a person or animal lives that they want to protect against strangers

trespassing to enter somewhere without permission

underpass a tunnel under a road or railway for people on foot; a subway

valuables your treasured belongings such as your purse, wallet, jewellery, watch or gadgets

FURTHER INFORMATION

Websites

www.beatbullying.org
If you are experiencing bullying inside or outside of school, this website will give you lots of advice on what to do and who to talk to.

bikeability.dft.gov.uk/
Cycling courses designed to give you the skills and confidence to cycle on the road.

www.kidshealth.org/kid/watch
Loads of advice about how to stay safe.

www.safestreet.info
A website produced by the West Midlands Police, with interactive challenges and lots of information.

www.trackoff.org/Dangers.aspx
A look at why trains and train tracks are dangerous, with facts and a video from a train driver's point of view.

Books

Kidpower Safety Comics, **Irene van der Zande and Kidpower International**, CreateSpace Independent Publishing Platform, 2012

The Willow Street Kids: Be Smart Stay Safe, **Michele Elliott**, Macmillan Children's Books, 1997

What Would You Do?, **Linda Schwartz**, Creative Teaching Press, 2011

Helplines

Childline 0800 1111
Childline is a helpline for young people who need to talk about problems.

Emergency Services 999
The emergency number connects you to the police, ambulance service or fire brigade. Dial this number if there is a serious crime taking place, or if someone's life is in danger or a threat of violence to you or someone else. It's a free call from a mobile or land line.

Non-emergency Police 101
Call this non-emergency number if you see someone behaving oddly, if you want to report a crime, or if you want to talk to the police about anything. There is a small charge for this call.

INDEX

SERIES CONTENTS

Keeping Safe around Alcohol, Drugs and Cigarettes
- Avoiding Harm from Drink, Drugs and Cigarettes
- Being Around Drink, Drugs and Cigarettes
- About Alcohol • Alcohol Around You • Alcohol and You
- Cigarettes and Addiction • Dangers of Smoking
- Avoiding Smoke • About Drugs • Dangers of Drug Misuse
- Dangers to You • Taking a Stand

Keeping Safe on the Street
- Be Street Smart • Know Your Journey
- Stay Aware • Dog Dangers • Stranger Danger
- Trouble on the Streets • Safe Cycling
- Safe Skateboarding • Keep Away from Building Sites
- Keep Away from Rail Tracks
- Stay Safe on Public Transport • After Dark

Keeping Safe Online
- Having a Happy Online Life • Cyberbullying
- Using Social Media Safely • Share Carefully
- Keep Your Information Safe • Online Chat
- Stay in Your Comfort Zone • Too Much
- Click With Care • Going Viral • Infected Computer
- Dealing With Problems

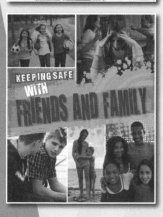

Keeping Safe with Friends and Family
- Making Decisions • Helping Out • Emergency!
- Anger and Arguments • Family Matters • Pet Safety
- Peer Pressure • Safety at Home • Out with Friends
- Going to Friends' Houses • Your Body Belongs to You
- Good Secrets and Bad Secrets